LEARN ENGLISH

Everyday

GREETING

Author Lynn Franklin

Copyright © 2020 by Lynn Franklin. All Rights Reserved.

No part of this publication may be reproduced, distributed, or transmitted in any form or by any means, including photocopying, recording, or other electronic or mechanical methods, or by any information storage and retrieval system without the prior written permission of the author, except in the case of very brief quotations embodied in critical reviews and certain other noncommercial uses permitted by copyright law.

GREETING

Basic patterns.

Hello.

Good morning.

How are you doing?

Not bad.

What's up?

It's nice to meet you.

It's nice to see you again.

I'm surprised to see you here.

Long time no see

How have you been?

Hi there.

How are things with you?

What's going on with you?

What are you doing here?

Hey.

Dialogue one.

Good morning. Good morning to you too. Do you think it will rain today? Yeah, maybe it's hard to tell.

I hope not. I am going to the store this afternoon. Maybe you should check the weather forecast first. Good idea. I think I will. Well, I hope you have a good afternoon. You too.

john

dialogue two

Hello. Hello, Frank How are you doing? Not bad. Work is going well. Oh, isn't that's good to hear. What about you?

 I'm doing okay. Although my car's in the shop. Oh, really? That's too bad.

Dialogue three.

Hi, John. Oh, hey, Willie, did you have a good time hiking today? Yes. Although it was a bit hot. That is why I stayed inside. What did you do? I read a book.

dialog four

what's up, Anthony? Not much. Not much at all. Are you hungry

A little bit. Do you want to eat? Yes. Let's go find something to eat. That sounds good to me.

Dialogue five

Good afternoon is Dr. Hill busy? Yes, he is busy. Do you mind waiting? I don't mind. Do you think he will be a while? He shouldn't be long? Oh good. Oh wait, just take a seat over there. He should see you shortly.

Substitution drills.

Do you think it will rain today?

Do you think it will rain tomorrow?

Do you think it will rain tonight?

Do you think it will rain this afternoon

two

Hello, Frank Good afternoon, Frank. Good morning, Frank.

Good evening, Bill.

Three

Did you have a good time hiking today?

Did you have a good time reading today?

Did you have a good time walking today?

Did you have a good time swimming today

four

is Dr. Cold in

is Dr. King available

is Dr. King here

is Dr. King around.

Five

it's hard to tell it's tough to tell. It's difficult to tell. It's not easy to tell.

Six

Oh, hey, Mark.

Oh, hi, Mark.

Oh, hello, Mark.

Oh, good morning, Mark.

Seven

Yes. Although it was a bit hot.

Yes. Although it was a bit cold.

Yes. Although it was a bit wet.

Yes, although it was a bit cloudy

eight

I read a book.

I read a magazine.

I read a story.

I read a poem

nine.

I am going to the beach this afternoon.

I am going to the park this afternoon.

I am going to the library this afternoon. I am going to the store this afternoon

10

That is why I stayed inside.

That is why I stayed indoors. That is why I stayed in the shade. That is why I stayed in

11

how are you doing? How are things? How are you feeling? How are you?

12

it's hard to tell.

It's hard to know.

It's hard to say. It's hard to be sure.

13

I'm doing okay. Although my car is in the shop. I'm doing well. Although my car is in the shop. I'm doing good. Although my car is in the shop. I'm doing fine. Although my car is in the shop

14

I'm doing okay. Hold on.

My car is in the shop.

I'm doing okay. Although my bike is in the shop. I'm doing okay.   Although my boat is in the shop.   I'm doing okay. Although my guitar is in the shop

15

maybe you should check the weather forecast first. Maybe you should watch the weather forecast first. Maybe you should listen to the weather forecast first. Maybe you should see the weather forecast first.

monologue. Bill was not having a good day because his car was in the shop. A shop can mean a store, but it originally meant a place to make or repair things.

In that sense, Bill means his car is being repaired.

It can be difficult to not have a car in America for many people.

In large cities, it is not so important to have a car. In cities, public transportation, such as buses is available for people to use. In fact, many city people prefer not to have a car.

outside the city though, having a car is often necessary for many jobs and routine tasks. buying food, going to the library or seeing friends are often difficult to do without a car. automobiles are an important part of American life.

DISCLAMER STATEMENT

All information and content contained in this book are provided solely for general information and reference purposes. SSP LLC Limited makes no statement, representation, warranty or guarantee as to the accuracy, reliability or timeliness of the information and content contained in this Book.

Neither SSP Limited or the author of this book nor any of its related company accepts any responsibility or liability for any direct or indirect loss or damage (whether in tort, contract or otherwise) which may be suffered or occasioned by any person howsoever arising due to any inaccuracy, omission, misrepresentation or error in respect of any information and content provided by this book (including any third-party books.

NOTES

NOTES

NOTES

NOTES

NOTES

NOTES

NOTES

NOTES

NOTES

NOTES

NOTES

www.ingramcontent.com/pod-product-compliance
Lightning Source LLC
Chambersburg PA
CBHW052130110526
44592CB00013B/1826